Plank It!
Wrap It!

Tiffany Haugen

A *Frank*
mato
PORTLAND

To my best wood chopper

Spiral-bound ISBN-13: 978-1-57188-414-5
Spiral-bound UPC: 0-81127-00248-1
Book Design: Esther Poleo Design
Photography: Tiffany Haugen
Printed in Hong Kong

Published in 2007 by
FRANK AMATO PUBLICATIONS, INC.
PO Box 82112 • Portland, Oregon 9728
(503) 653-8108 • www.amatobooks.com

▲ Appetizers 14

▲ Vegetables 19

▲ Meat 24

▲ Fish & Seafood 34

▲ Desserts 40

▲ Wrap It! 43

▲ Marinades, Rubs & More 49

Contents

Introduction

The process of cooking food on cut wood dates back to Native American cultures on both the East and West coasts of North America. This style of cooking results in tender, juicy, delectable foods, ranging from meats to desserts. Today, plank cooking and cooking with wood papers (wraps) has been refined to meet the needs of modern-day appliances, such as grills, barbecues and ovens.

Woods that have been cut, planed, sanded and sometimes kiln-dried, present abundant opportunities in which food can be prepared. Growing in popularity among restaurants and culinary institutes the world over, cooking on wood infuses food with a rich, smokey essence. Rather than waiting for smoke-cured meats to enjoy the flavor natural woods have to offer, now, by cooking on a plank or wrap, the alluring taste is only minutes away.

The flavor of many foods, both savory and sweet, are dramatically accentuated when

cooked on wood. In addition, an appealing, ready-to-serve presentation can be attained directly from the grill or oven. To many people, the novelty of preparing food on a plank or wrap is especially enjoyable for both indoor and outdoor entertainment, no matter what the time of year.

This book contains many recipes and handling techniques unique to plank cooking and cooking with wood papers. All recipes can be interchanged—plank recipes will work on wraps and vice versa. Wood wraps are not suitable for cooking times over 30 minutes and should not be used over direct heat. Plank recipes can be halved or quartered to fit on smaller wraps. Almost any recipe can be adapted to cook on a plank or wrap; the fun is in the experimentation.

Once the basics of plank cooking and cooking with wraps are mastered, a whole new world of preparing food presents itself. When you discover the scrumptious flavors and exquisite textures that cooking on wood has to offer, you'll be glad you learned the techniques sooner rather than later.

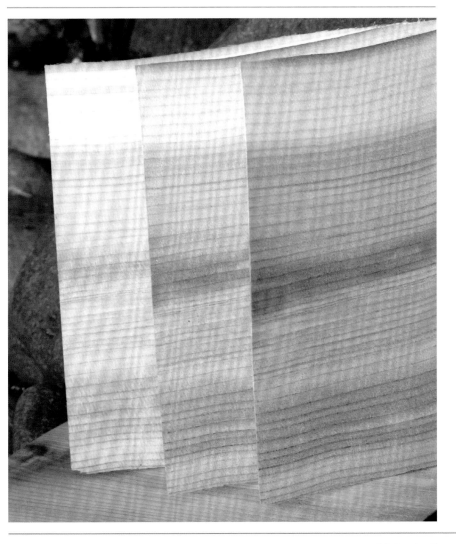

Getting Started

What To Look For In A Plank

The more plank cooking you do, the more versed you'll become at targeting what tastes are most appealing. If you do a great deal of plank cooking, you may wish to explore outside the realm of the woods most commonly used; then again, you may be pleased with stockpiling general woods like cedar or alder.

When cooking on a plank, avoid using resinous woods such as pine, fir, juniper or poplar as these and other woods like them may contain volatile oils. If buying wood direct from a lumber yard or building supply store, be certain the woods have not been treated with any chemicals. You want either kiln or naturally dried hardwoods to cook on.

If you have access to raw wood—trees you can fall and split yourself—you'll find these natural wood *"sections"* make good planking material. Western red cedar, alder, maple and oak are some of the most commonly used woods in raw form, straight from the tree. The key to obtaining a good-quality, raw cooking plank is storing the split segments in a dry place where they can naturally cure without mold forming.

Due to convenience and safety purposes, many people elect to purchase prepackaged woods, ready to cook, from commercial producers of the product.

The more plank-proficient you become, the more you'll want to experiment with different wood types. Deriving individual wood flavors can be accomplished by soaking planks in different liquids, but for a true change of taste, cooking on different species of wood is the best way to find variety.

When obtaining planks, be sure the dimensions of the wood will fit inside your grill or oven, prior to cooking—if you have a way to cut larger planks to size, this is no concern. You'll also want to make sure that, prior to placing food on the plank, it will fit. The edges of planks tend to burn, so be certain the food can be situated on the plank with an inch or so to spare on all sides.

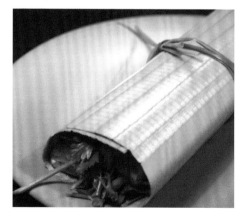

What To Look For In A Wrap

New to many cooks, wood papers or wraps are quickly finding their way to many specialty food stores and can be attained from many

Internet sites. Wraps are different from planks in that they are much thinner, and not meant to ever catch fire to produce smoke. Using a presoaked wrap helps to keep food moist while imparting a woodsy essence. Wraps can be used rolled or flat, in the oven or on the grill, over indirect heat.

Wraps can be found in several wood flavors. Cedar and alder are the most common but apple, maple and cherry are also available. Follow the same guidelines for choosing plank flavors when choosing wood wraps.

Unless you have special wood-working equipment that allows you to cut paper-thin sheets of wood, your best bet is purchasing the wraps.

Please note: All recipes in the plank section can be halved or quartered and cooked in a grilling paper. Wraps can be used flat, like a plank, and cooked over indirect heat on the grill or in the oven.

SOAKING & SEASONING PLANKS AND WRAPS FOR COOKING

Prior to cooking with any plank or wrap, it should first be soaked. Soaking serves several purposes, the main goal being to foster the absorption of fluids which ultimately keeps food moist when cooking. This allows food to retain valued nutrients and results in a more distinct taste quality. In addition to keeping foods from drying out, soaking planks helps food cook evenly. This means food won't get overdone on the edges, while only partially cooked in the middle. The only exception to the soaking rule is if the plank is to be used in the oven to prepare a quick cooking food such as garlic bread or a very thin fillet of fish.

Soaking wood prior to cooking also reduces its burn rate when placed on the grill. The end result is a nice, woody smoke essence versus a harsh smoke flavor which can come from cooking on dry or charred wood.

If soaked and closely managed during the cooking process, some planks may be used repeatedly. Some of the harder woods, like oak or maple, can be used many times if properly cared for. Planks used in the oven can last through dozens of cookings, as they are not exposed to direct flames. Wraps can only be used one time; always dispose of them after initial use.

While water is the most common liquid in which to soak planks and wraps, fruit juices, vinegar, wine and other alcohols can also be used. Fully submerging a plank or wrap in these mediums imparts light flavors of the liquids into the foods being cooked. If wishing to tone down the flavor of the liquids which planks are soaked in, mix them with water.

Soaking times for planks can range from one to 24 hours, with one hour being the minimum. Wraps only need to soak 10-15 minutes. Depending on the size and type of wood, as well as personal preference, soaking times can vary. Tight-grained, larger planks can soak longer than thin, more open-grained woods.

Once soaked, remove the plank and place it on the grill, cooking side down, at medium heat and allow it to dry out and preheat for five minutes; be careful not to let the plank catch fire. If cooking in the house, place plank in a 350° oven for 10 minutes. Once heated in the grill or oven, brush a light coating of olive oil onto the cooking side of the board. The oil will season the wood for cooking, keep food from sticking to the wood and help the food retain moisture and nutrients.

Getting Started

WRAPS SHOULD NOT BE DRIED PRIOR TO COOKING. ALWAYS PLACE FOOD TO BE COOKED ON SOAKED WRAPS.

If looking for additional flavor, rub a clove of garlic over both sides of the dried plank or wet wrap. You can also lay a bed of fresh herbs, vegetables or fruits on the cooking side of the plank or wrap, placing the food to be cooked on top.

Wraps, narrow planks, and regular-sized planks that have been cut down in size, are great for dinner parties, with participants creating their own plank-cooked meals. Here, the food of choice, be it a fish fillet or veggies, can be dressed in herbs, spices, rubs or sauces by each individual. Each custom-created plank or wrap can be cooked simultaneously, and in the end, everyone can sit down and enjoy their special meal together.

WORDS OF CAUTION

When cooking on a plank or wrap, never leave the area unattended. When cooking on a grill, avoid repeatedly opening the cover as this can cause flare-ups and lost heat. When opening the grill, do not stand directly over the unit, as smoke and heat will escape. Be careful not to inhale smoke or allow it to billow into the eyes. Always cook wraps over indirect heat.

When cooking fatty foods, note their tendency to cause flare-ups in the bottom of the grill, even on the plank itself. By close monitoring during the cooking process, excessive flare-ups can be kept in check.

When the plank begins to smoke, check to prevent undue flare-ups. Use a spray bottle filled with water to extinguish any flame on the plank. This approach not only prevents overcooking, it promotes a more robust flavor due to increased smoke production.

If serving food directly off a plank or wrap, or moving either with the food still on it, be certain to place it on a safe surface. The underside of the wood is extremely hot and can cause some surfaces to melt or catch fire. Having a large metal spatula with which to lift and transport the wood is a good idea and allows for easy placement onto a large plate. Take care not to bring a burning or even a smoldering plank or wrap inside the house.

If removing food from the plank while on the grill, be sure to also remove the plank from the grill surface. It's good practice to immediately douse the hot plank in water, by either running it under an outside faucet or submerging it in a bucket of water.

KNOW YOUR GRILL

Plank cooking is one of those undertakings that is best mastered through repeated practice. One of the key steps is getting to know your grill and how it performs. Whether you cook on a side-by-side or front-to-back burner grill, or cook on a charcoal barbecue, it's critical to learn where the hotspots are. Some portions of the grill may burn hotter than others, which can greatly aid in the cooking of your food should you require more or less heat.

Grilling units featuring temperature-control devices are convenient, but not necessary. A standing temperature gauge works well, is

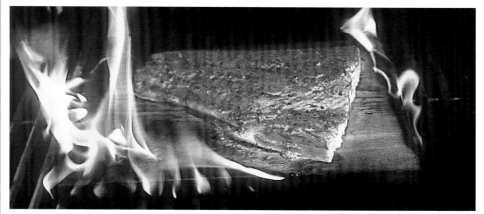

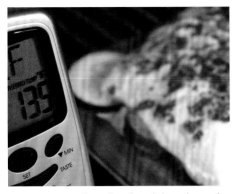

inexpensive, and can be placed directly on the plank when cooking to give the truest reading of the unit temperature. A meat thermometer is a must, especially when cooking large cuts of meat such as a whole chicken, beef roast or pork loin.

When cooking over direct heat on the grill, that is, where the food is placed on the lowest rack, directly over the flame, use a low setting-if not the lowest setting possible. Cook with the lid closed so smoke completely engulfs the food to infuse flavor. The goal is to reach a level of heavy smoke in 15-20 minutes; doing so any sooner can result in uneven heating, likely burning the outer edges of the food. Once the plank begins to smoke, check often, spray bottle in hand, to extinguish any flames on the plank. This method promotes a strong smoke flavor.

When cooking over indirect heat on the grill, where food is placed away from the flame or in a hanging basket, use a medium heat setting. If using charcoal, pile the coals to one side and place plank opposite or elevated above the heat source. Cook with the lid closed, so the smoke surrounds the food to infuse flavor. Here, the plank should begin to smoke after 15-20 minutes. The plank should not catch fire when cooking over indirect heat. This method promotes a light smoke flavor, and takes longer to cook foods due to a lower overall internal temperature.

When grilling outside, weather conditions can be ever-changing, thus impacting cooking times. Outside temperature, humidity levels, even wind direction can impact the cooking rate of a grill. Cooking temperatures on the grill should range between 350-450 degrees. Knowing the anatomy of your grill and how it responds to varying climatic and seasonal conditions is important, and easy to learn with time.

COOKING WITH PLANKS AND WRAPS IN THE OVEN

Cooking with planks and wraps in the oven is a great option. Though this approach is easy to maintain control over, it does not attain the concentrated smoke flavors achieved on the outside grill. Nonetheless, it is a very popular way of cooking, and it does impart a gentle woody essence into foods. One of the most appealing qualities to inside planking is the attractive aroma it introduces into the house.

For plank cooking, begin by preheating the oven and the presoaked plank, together, to 350°. Once oven has been preheated, oil the plank,

place food on plank and put directly on oven rack. It's a good idea to position a foil-lined baking sheet on the rack below the plank, to catch any drippings. Planks cooked in the oven can be used repeatedly. There are special, oven-only planks on the market, complete with internal adjustment rods to control warping. These specialized oven planks are considerably thicker when compared to grilling-style planks and can be pricey, but the extended cooking opportunities they promote make them a good value.

Many foods, such as fish, seafood and vegetables, benefit from a moist cooking environment. It is easy to apply this technique when plank cooking in the oven. Simply place plank in a shallow, ovenproof pan, partially submerging it in water or other liquids; do not let the liquids touch the food on the plank. Additional liquid may be added during the cooking to keep the plank moist and steaming.

When done cooking on a plank, be it in the oven or on the grill, quickly cool the plank. This will preserve the plank, ensuring it doesn't continue to cook or smolder on the underside, or internally. Cleaning the plank is the final step, if looking to reuse it. Thoroughly wash with warm water and mild dish soap. A solution of one part bleach to nine parts water can also be used to clean and sterilize a plank. Scrub to make sure all fat residues are removed and store the plank in a dry place, so molds do not form.

When reusing a plank that has become overly darkened, go over the cooking side with sand paper. Planks used in the oven can become laden with oils, masking the natural wood flavor. Sanding will recharge the plank, exposing fresh wood which allows for even cooking temperatures and better-tasting food. Be sure to soak the plank prior to each cooking session, and always preheat the plank which not only makes for more efficient cooking, but also sterilizes it.

▍ WOOD TYPES

Wraps (wood papers) are commonly found in cedar and alder but are now available in apple, maple and cherry. Use the same flavor guidelines as given for plank flavors.

Pecan

Cherry

Maple

Oak

PLEASE NOTE: WOOD TYPES ARE SUGGESTED IN EVERY RECIPE, BUT DO NOT LIMIT YOURSELF; EXPERIMENT AND FIND OUT WHAT FLAVORS SUIT YOUR TASTES BEST.

THE MOST COMMON PLANKING WOODS

ALDER: Common in the Pacific Northwest, gives off a delicate smokey flavor that is slightly sweet. Recommended for fish, poultry, pork and vegetables.

CEDAR: One of the most diverse, Western red cedar produces a deep yet lenient wood flavor. Recommended for fish, pork, beef and any foods with bold spicy flavors.

OTHER FLAVORS READILY AVAILABLE

APPLE: Preferred for its mild, fruity flavor with a hint of sweetness. Recommended for all smoked foods. Great also as a blend with stronger woods such as hickory and mesquite.

Apricot: A mild, sweet fruit wood. Recommended for pork and poultry.

BIRCH: Similar to the fruit woods. Recommended for pork and poultry.

CHERRY: Slightly sweet and fruity, this mellow wood is great for blending with stronger woods. Recommended most for poultry, this wood can be used with all foods.

HICKORY: The most common wood used for smoking, bold and sometimes peppery with a hint of sweetness. Recommended most for pork, chicken and beef, also flavors well with mesquite.

LEMON: Stronger smoke flavor, citrus woods pair well with milder woods.

MAPLE: One of the most versatile smoking woods, mild and slightly sweet, flavors can vary in different regions. Recommended for vegetables and all other smoked foods.

MESQUITE: Perfect for a short time on the grill, strong and tangy. Recommended most for beef, vegetables, pork and poultry, goes well with hickory.

NECTARINE & PEACH: Similar to pecan and the fruit woods. Recommended for pork, poultry and beef.

PEAR: Similar to apple, a mild, sweet fruit wood. Recommended for all smoked foods. Great also as a blend with stronger woods such as hickory and mesquite.

PECAN: Common in the South, pecan is a versatile, mellow smoke flavor. Recommended for all smoked foods. Great also as a blend with stronger woods such as hickory and mesquite.

OAK: One of the most common fuels, oak has a subtle flavor that goes with a variety of foods and lends itself well to blending with stronger smoking woods. Recommended for all smoked foods.

HELPFUL TIPS

For easy serving sizes, precut fish to the skin in the desired serving size. Place slices of lemons, limes or oranges, or perhaps herb leaves or sliced garlic, in the cut between each serving portion.

Placing meat or fish on a bed of vegetables, fruit or herbs, helps heat and smoke penetrate more evenly. The food placed underneath stays moist and acquires a great smoke flavor.

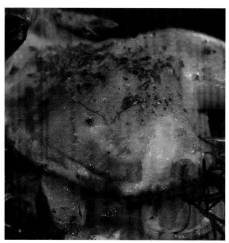

Always control flare-ups immediately. The goal with plank cooking is to bathe food in smoke, not burn up the plank.

For easier handling, if space allows, foil can be placed at the end of a plank to keep the area from excessive charring.

Bathing food in rich smoke flavors is the goal of outdoor plank cooking. Even foods that cook a short time will take-on tastes from plank cooking.

Several planks/wraps can be used at one time on the grill. Keep adequate space between each plank for airflow, and always watch food closely. Control all flare-ups immediately.

WRAP PREPARATION

STEPS

1. Soak wrap in water or suggested liquid 10-15 minutes.

2. Place food on moist wrap, roll closed and secure with a metal clip or kitchen twine.

3. Always cook on indirect heat on a grill and do not cook in an oven exceeding 350°.

Soak wrap in water.

Secure with a metal clip or kitchen twine.

PLANK PREPARATION

STEPS

1. Soak plank in water or suggested liquid, minimum 1 hour, maximum 24 hours.

2. Preheat plank on grill at medium heat 5 minutes, or in a 350° oven 10 minutes.

3. Brush a light coating of olive oil onto cooking side of board.

PLANK COOKING OPTIONS

GRILL (DIRECT HEAT): Use the lowest setting on a gas grill or low charcoal heat. Place plank with food directly over the heat source. Cook with the lid closed so smoke surrounds food and infuses flavor. Plank should reach heavy smoke in 15-20 minutes. When plank begins to smoke, check often—use spray bottle filled with water to extinguish any flame on the plank. This method promotes a heavy smoke flavor.

GRILL (INDIRECT HEAT): Use a medium setting on a gas grill. If using charcoal, pile coals to one side. Place plank opposite the heat source. Cook with lid closed so smoke surrounds food and infuses flavor. Plank should begin to smoke after 15-20 minutes.

The plank should not catch fire using this method. Cooking time increases due to the lower temperature. This method promotes a light smoke flavor.

OVEN: Preheat oven and board to 350° or as stated in recipe. Place plank with food, directly on oven rack. Position a foil-lined baking sheet on the rack below the plank to catch any drippings. This method infuses a light smoke essence into food. Planks can be reused.

WARNING: When cooking, never leave planks unattended. Avoid repeatedly opening grill cover as this can cause flare-ups and lost heat. When opening grill, take caution not to inhale or stand in direct smoke.

Appetizers

Caramelized Veggies & Brie |

Heat olive oil in medium skillet on medium-high heat. Sauté onions and peppers 10-15 minutes. Add sugar and vinegar and cook an additional 10 minutes, stirring frequently. Remove from heat, add salt and pepper. Place cheese wedge on prepared plank, topping with sautéed vegetables. Grill or bake at 350° until cheese is warm and beginning to melt, serve immediately with bread, crackers or tortilla chips.

INGREDIENTS
- 1 7-ounce wedge brie cheese
- 2 tablespoons olive oil
- 1 cup onion, thinly sliced
- 1 bell pepper, thinly sliced
- 2 teaspoons sugar
- 2 teaspoons cider vinegar
- 1/2 teaspoon salt
- 1/4 teaspoon white pepper

1 prepared plank, maple, oak or alder, soaked in white wine or water (See page 13, **Plank Preparation**).

Confetti Sausage Balls |

INGREDIENTS
- 1 pound seasoned sausage
- 1/2 cup biscuit baking mix
- 1 egg
- 1/2 cup fresh spinach, finely chopped
- 1/4 cup pineapple, finely chopped
- 1/4 cup red bell pepper, finely chopped

1 prepared plank, maple, oak or alder, soaked in white wine or water (See page 13, **Plank Preparation**).

RECIPE VARIATION
Substitute diced green chilies for pineapple and sundried tomatoes for bell pepper. For cheesy sausage balls, add 1/2 cup of any grated or crumbled cheese.

In a large bowl, mix all ingredients until well blended. Do not over mix. Shape into balls using one heaping tablespoon of meat mixture. Place balls on prepared plank. Grill or bake at 375° 20-25 minutes or until internal temperature reaches 160°.

Hazelnut Cheese Bites |

INGREDIENTS

- 1 1/4 cups bread crumbs
- 1 cup cheddar cheese, grated
- 1/2 cup hazelnuts, ground
- 1 tablespoon flour
- 2 green onions, finely chopped
- 2 tablespoons fresh parsley, finely chopped
- 1 teaspoon dry mustard
- 1/2 teaspoon salt
- 1/4 teaspoon white pepper
- 2 eggs, well beaten
- 2 tablespoons milk
- 2 tablespoons melted butter
- Melted butter for brushing

1 prepared plank, cedar, alder or fruit wood (See page 13, **Plank Preparation**).

In a medium bowl, mix all dry ingredients until thoroughly combined. In a small bowl, beat eggs until frothy and add remaining ingredients. Add egg mixture to dry ingredients and stir until blended. Divide mixture into 15-20 balls and form into desired shape. Place cheese bites on prepared plank and brush with melted butter. Grill or bake at 375° 15-20 minutes or until lightly browned.

RECIPE VARIATION

Substitute pepper jack cheese for cheddar cheese. Substitute a favorite pesto for the parsley and dry mustard. Any nuts can be used for the hazelnuts.

Crab Cakes |

INGREDIENTS

- 1 pound crab meat
- 1 cup seasoned bread crumbs
- 1 egg, beaten
- 1/4 cup mayonnaise
- 1 teaspoon Worcestershire sauce
- 1/2 teaspoon dry mustard
- 1/2 teaspoon salt
- 1/4 teaspoon pepper
- Melted butter for brushing

1 prepared plank, cedar, alder or fruit wood (See page 13, **Plank Preparation**).

In a medium bowl, combine all ingredients except for the crab. Gently mix in crab. If mixture is too dry to form cakes, add more mayonnaise. Shape mixture into small cakes. Place crab cakes on prepared plank and brush with melted butter. Grill or bake at 375° 10-15 minutes or until lightly browned. Flip cakes over once during cooking. Serve with Spicy Sauce or Green Sauce (page 51).

RECIPE VARIATION

Substitute 1 cup cooked corn and jalapeños for crab. Any cooked and deboned fish can be used instead of crab.

Curried Drop-Meatballs with Raita

INGREDIENTS
- 1 pound ground pork, turkey or lamb
- 2 green onions
- 1/4 cup yogurt
- 1/4 cup ground almonds
- 1/4 cup oatmeal or oat bran
- 2 tablespoons fresh mint, finely chopped
- 1 tablespoon olive oil
- 3 cloves garlic, crushed
- Juice and zest of 1 lemon
- 1 teaspoon curry powder
- 1/2 teaspoon salt
- 1/2 teaspoon ground cardamom or coriander
- 1/4 teaspoon cayenne pepper

In a large bowl, mix all ingredients until well blended. Do not over mix. Using two spoons to shape, drop meat mixture by rounded spoonfuls onto prepared plank. Grill or bake at 375° 20-25 minutes or until internal temperature reaches 160°.

1 prepared plank, alder or fruit wood (See page13, **Plank Preparation**).

CUCUMBER RAITA
- 3/4 cup plain yogurt
- 1 large cucumber, peeled and diced
- Juice of 1/2 lemon
- 1/4 cup finely chopped fresh chives
- 1/4 teaspoon salt

In a medium bowl, gently combine all ingredients.

Shrimp Puffs

INGREDIENTS
- 3 tablespoons butter
- 1/3 cup shallots or onions, diced
- 1/2 cup mushrooms, finely chopped
- 1/3 cup green olives, finely chopped
- 1 cup bay or salad shrimp
- 1/2 cup sour cream
- 1/4 cup feta cheese, crumbled
- 10 sheets prepared phyllo dough (approximately 9" x 14")
- 1/4 cup melted butter, for brushing

1 prepared plank, alder or fruit wood (See page 13, **Plank Preparation**).

RECIPE VARIATION
Crab meat or ground sausage can be substituted for shrimp. Substitute capers or black olives for green olives.

In a small skillet, sauté shallots and mushrooms in butter until soft. Cool completely. In a medium bowl, gently combine remaining ingredients. Place one sheet of phyllo on a cutting board. Brush sheet with melted butter, top with a second sheet of phyllo. Cut the double layer of phyllo into 3 equal sections, lengthwise. Place a tablespoon of shrimp filling at the bottom of a section. Diagonally fold phyllo over the filling, taking corner to the opposite edge, like folding a flag. Continue folding, keeping the triangle shape all the way to end. Place puffs, seam side down, on prepared plank. Brush the tops of the puffs with melted butter. Grill or bake at 375° 15-20 minutes or until triangles are golden brown. Shrimp Puffs may be prepared in advance and refrigerated, add 5 minutes to cooking time.

Little Smokeys with BBQ Sauce |

INGREDIENTS

- 1 pound ground beef
- 1/2 cup soda cracker crumbs
- 1 egg
- 2 tablespoons onion, minced
- 2 teaspoons Worcestershire sauce
- 1/2 teaspoon salt
- 1/4 teaspoon black pepper

1 prepared plank, cedar or hickory, soaked in red wine or water (See page 13, **Plank Preparation**).

BBQ SAUCE

- 1/4 cup ketchup
- 1 tablespoon red wine vinegar
- 1 tablespoon Worcestershire sauce
- 1 tablespoon honey
- 1/2 tablespoon Dijon mustard
- 1/4 teaspoon salt
- 1/4 teaspoon liquid hickory smoke, optional
- 3-10 dashes hot pepper sauce

In a large bowl, mix all ingredients until well blended. Do not over mix. Shape into balls using one heaping tablespoon of meat mixture. Place meatballs on prepared plank and brush with BBQ Sauce several times while cooking. Grill or bake at 375° 20-25 minutes or until internal temperature reaches 160°.

In a small bowl, mix BBQ sauce ingredients until thoroughly combined.

Vegetables

Orzo-Stuffed Peppers |

INGREDIENTS

▮ 4 large red, yellow, orange or green bell peppers
▮ 2 tablespoons olive oil
▮ 1/4 cup onion, diced
▮ 2 cloves garlic, minced
▮ 1 1/4 cups orzo pasta, uncooked
▮ 1 cup fresh spinach, chopped
▮ 1 14.5-ounce can chicken broth
▮ 1/2 teaspoon Italian seasoning
▮ Olive oil for drizzling

1 prepared plank, cedar, pecan or fruit wood, soaked in white wine or water (See page 13, **Plank Preparation**).

RECIPE VARIATION

For a complete meal add 1 cup cooked and seasoned ground beef, turkey or sausage to the orzo stuffing.

Wash and dry peppers. Cut tops off peppers and discard all seeds. Set aside. In a large skillet, sauté onion and garlic in olive oil 3-6 minutes. Add orzo and stir until lightly browned. Add remaining ingredients and simmer until liquid is absorbed. Fill peppers with orzo mixture. Arrange peppers on prepared plank and drizzle olive oil over peppers. Grill or bake at 375° 35-40 minutes or until peppers are tender.

Zucchini Parmesan |

INGREDIENTS

▮ 2-4 zucchini, cut into strips
▮ 1/3 cup Italian dressing or
▮ Rosemary Balsamic Marinade (page 50)
▮ 1/2 cup corn flakes, crushed
▮ 1/3 cup parmesan cheese, grated
▮ 2 tablespoons butter, melted

1 prepared plank, alder, oak or fruit wood (See page 13, **Plank Preparation**).
Place cut zucchini into a sealable plastic bag. Add dressing and let marinate at least 15 minutes. In a small bowl mix corn flakes, cheese and butter until thoroughly combined. Arrange zucchini strips on a prepared plank. Take care not to stack the strips more than two high. Sprinkle with corn flake mixture and grill or bake at 375° 15-25 minutes or until topping is toasted and zucchini is tender.

Red Potatoes with Blue Cheese |

INGREDIENTS
- 8-10 small red potatoes
- 1/2 cup blue cheese, crumbled
- Salt and pepper to taste

1 prepared plank, cedar, hickory or fruit wood (See page 13, **Plank Preparation**).

Wash and dry potatoes. Place potatoes in a foil pouch and bake at 350° for 30 minutes, or until slightly soft. Remove from oven and cool to the touch. Make a small cut in the top of each potato and squeeze open. Top potatoes with salt, pepper and blue cheese. Place on prepared plank and grill or bake at 375° 10-15 minutes.

RECIPE VARIATION
Substitute baking potatoes for red potatoes and fill with desired fillings (cheese, chili, sautéed vegetables, bacon, chives and/or sour cream). Plank cook until toppings are warmed throughout.

Shrimp-Stuffed Portabellas |

INGREDIENTS
- 4-6 portobello mushrooms or 12-20 small mushrooms
- 1/2 cup cheddar cheese, grated
- 1/2 cup parmesan cheese, grated
- 1/2 cup mayonnaise
- 1/2 cup black olives, sliced
- 1/2 cup cooked bay or salad shrimp

1 prepared plank, cedar, oak or alder, soaked in white wine or water (See page 13, **Plank Preparation**).

RECIPE VARIATION
This filling works well with small button or crimini mushrooms; reduce cooking time to 10-15 minutes. Chopped spinach or broccoli can be substituted for the shrimp.

Clean mushrooms with a damp towel or mushroom brush. Remove stems and finely chop. In a medium bowl mix cheeses with mayonnaise. Gently fold in olives, shrimp and mushroom stems. Brush both sides of mushrooms with olive oil. Salt and pepper both sides. Fill with stuffing mixture. Place stuffed mushrooms on a prepared plank. Grill or bake at 375° 20-25 minutes or until cheese mixture is bubbly and mushrooms are tender.

Tofu & Vegetable Kebabs |

INGREDIENTS
I 1 14.5-ounce package extra-firm tofu
I Spicy Sauce (page 51) or
  Teriyaki Marinade (page 50)

USE ANY COMBINATION OF THE FOLLOWING VEGETABLES

I Red or yellow onion
I Yellow squash
I Zucchini squash
I Red bell pepper
I Green bell pepper
I Yellow bell pepper
I Cherry tomatoes
I Mushrooms

Metal or wooden skewers (soak wooden skewers at least 1 hour in water)
1 prepared plank, alder, oak or fruit wood (See page 13, **Plank Preparation**).

Remove tofu from package and press into paper towels to remove excess moisture. Cut to bite-sized pieces. Place tofu in marinade or sauce of choice and marinate at least 20 minutes. Cut vegetables into bite-sized pieces and marinate if desired or simply brush with olive oil. Thread vegetables and tofu on skewers. Place on a prepared plank. Grill or bake at 375° 20-25 minutes or until vegetables reach desired tenderness. Baste with marinade while grilling if desired.

RECIPE VARIATION
Almost any vegetable can be prepared on a plank. For best results, steam or microwave vegetables that need longer cooking times prior to plank cooking.

Stuffed Sweet Potatoes |

INGREDIENTS

I 3-4 orange-fleshed sweet potatoes
I 1 15-ounce can baked beans
I 1 15-ounce can kidney or pinto beans,
  drained and rinsed
I 1 8-ounce can crushed pineapple, drained
I 1/4 cup green pepper or green
  chilies, diced
I 2 tablespoons yellow mustard
I 5-10 dashes hot pepper sauce
I Salt and pepper to taste

Wash and dry potatoes. Bake at 350° for 30-45 minutes, or until slightly soft. Remove from oven and cool to the touch. Cut potatoes in half lengthwise, scooping out the middle of the potato. Make the center of the potato deeper to hold the topping. Set scooped out potato aside to use for pancakes or muffins. In a medium bowl combine crushed pineapple, green pepper, mustard and hot pepper sauce. Mix until thoroughly blended. Gently stir in baked and kidney or pinto beans. Salt and pepper to taste. Place sweet potatoes on prepared plank. Evenly distribute bean mixture down the middle of the potatoes. Plank cook potatoes 15-20 minutes or until warmed throughout.

1 prepared plank, cedar, pecan or fruit wood, soaked in vinegar or water
(See page 13, **Plank Preparation**).

Cornbread-Stuffed Portabella Mushrooms |

INGREDIENTS

I 4-6 portabella mushrooms
I 1 tablespoon olive oil
I 1/4 cup celery, diced
I 1/4 cup bell pepper, diced
I 1/4 cup onion, diced
I 2 cloves garlic, minced
I 1/2 teaspoon tarragon, optional
I 2 cups cornbread, crumbled
I 1/2 cup parmesan cheese, grated
I Salt and pepper to taste
I 1/2 cup mozzarella cheese, optional

1 prepared plank, alder or fruit wood, soaked in white wine or water
(See page 13, **Plank Preparation**).

Clean mushrooms with a damp towel or mushroom brush. Remove stems and finely chop. Heat olive oil in medium skillet on medium-high heat. Sauté celery, peppers, onions and mushroom stems 7-10 minutes. Remove from heat, add garlic, tarragon, cornbread and parmesan cheese. Gently mix until combined. Brush both sides of mushrooms with olive oil. Salt and pepper both sides. Fill with stuffing mixture. Place stuffed mushrooms on a prepared plank. Grill or bake at 375° 25-30 minutes. Sprinkle with mozzarella cheese during last 10 minutes of cooking, if desired.

Meat

Garlic Roast with Onion Relish |

Puree garlic, sugar and spices in a food processor or mini-chopper. Pierce roast in many places with a fork. Coat roast completely with the garlic mixture. Marinate in the refrigerator 6-8 hours. Prior to cooking, let marinated roast sit at room temperature 30 minutes. Place on a prepared plank, cover loosely with foil, tucking ends of foil 1/2" under plank. Grill or bake at 350° 45 minutes to 1 hour or until desired doneness, 145° (medium-rare) to 170° (well-done). Let sit 10 minutes before slicing. Serve with Sweet Onion Relish.

SWEET ONION RELISH PREPARATION
In a medium bowl, mix all ingredients until thoroughly combined. Marinate, refrigerated at least 12 hours before serving for optimal flavor.

INGREDIENTS
▎ 1 1/2-pound beef roast or tri-tip
▎ 8-10 cloves garlic
▎ 1 tablespoon olive oil
▎ 1 tablespoon smoked paprika
▎ 1 tablespoon brown sugar
▎ 1 teaspoon black pepper
▎ 1 teaspoon salt

1 prepared plank, cedar or hickory, soaked in red wine or water (See page 13, **Plank Preparation**).

SWEET ONION RELISH
▎ 2 cups sweet onion, finely chopped
▎ 3 stalks celery, diced
▎ 1/3 cup sugar
▎ 2 tablespoons cider vinegar
▎ 1 teaspoon salt
▎ 1/2 teaspoon celery seed
▎ 1/4 teaspoon white pepper
▎ 1 2-ounce jar diced pimento

Stroganoff Tenderloin |

Ingredients

- 1 2-3-pound beef tenderloin
- Olive oil
- Salt and ground black pepper to taste

1 prepared plank, hickory or pecan,
soaked in wine, vinegar or water
(See page 13, **Plank Preparation**).

Stroganoff Gravy

- 4 tablespoons butter, divided
- 1 cup mushrooms,
  thinly sliced
- 2 tablespoons flour
- 1 can beef stock
- 1/4 cup red wine
- 2 tablespoons ketchup
- 1 tablespoon Dijon mustard
- 1/2 cup sour cream

Trim fat and silver skin from tenderloin. Rub meat with olive oil and salt and pepper to taste. On a hot grill, sear grill marks into every side of the tenderloin, 1-2 minutes per side. Place on a prepared plank. Grill or bake at 375° 30-40 minutes or until internal temperature reaches 145°. Remove from heat and cover with foil, keep roast on the plank. Let rest 10-15 minutes. Cut into thin slices and serve with Stroganoff Gravy or sauce of choice.

Stroganoff Gravy Preparation

In a medium skillet, sauté mushrooms in 2 tablespoons butter. Remove from pan, set aside. In the same skillet, melt 2 tablespoons butter on medium heat. Add flour and whisk, cooking until lightly browned. Slowly add beef stock, wine, ketchup and mustard. Whisk until thick and smooth, 4-6 minutes. Add sautéed mushrooms and sour cream. Remove from heat and serve immediately.

Horseradish-Stuffed Steak Rolls |

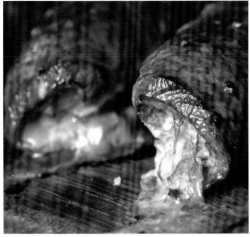

INGREDIENTS

▌ 1 pound beef steaks, thinly sliced
▌ 1 cup spinach, finely chopped
▌ 2 tablespoons creamy horseradish
▌ 3 cloves garlic, pureed
▌ 1/2 teaspoon dried thyme
▌ Salt and pepper to taste
▌ Olive oil for brushing

1 prepared plank, cedar or oak, soaked in white wine or water (See page 13, **Plank Preparation**).

RECIPE VARIATION

Substitute horseradish stuffing with cream cheese and Basil Pesto (page 51). Pounded, boneless, skinless chicken breasts can be substituted for beef.

Sprinkle both sides of thinly cut or pounded steaks with salt and pepper. In a medium bowl, combine all stuffing ingredients. Divide stuffing mixture equally among steaks. Roll steaks up, placing them seam-side down on prepared plank. Lightly brush with olive oil. Grill or bake at 375° 20-25 minutes or to desired doneness.

Pot Roast |

INGREDIENTS

▌ 1 2-pound chuck roast
▌ 1 onion, sliced
▌ 1-2 baking potatoes, sliced
▌ 3-4 carrots, peeled and halved
▌ Salt and pepper to taste
▌ Olive oil

1 prepared plank, cedar or fruit wood, soaked in water (See page 13, **Plank Preparation**).

Place onion slices on prepared plank. Steam cut potatoes and carrots 4-5 minutes in the microwave. Place on plank on top of onions. Salt and pepper to taste and brush lightly with olive oil. Season roast with salt and pepper, place atop potato and carrot layer. Cover loosely with foil, tucking ends of foil 1/2" under plank. Grill or bake at 350° 45 minutes to 1 hour or until desired doneness, 145° (medium-rare) to 170° (well-done). Remove foil during last 10 minutes of cooking time. Let sit 10 minutes before slicing.

Fajitas

INGREDIENTS

- 1 pound beef sirloin, sliced into strips
- 1 onion, sliced
- 1 green bell pepper, sliced
- 1 red or yellow bell pepper, sliced
- 1 portabello mushroom, sliced
- 2 tablespoons fajita seasoning mix or Basic Beef Rub (page 50) with 1 teaspoon cumin and 1/2 teaspoon chili powder added
- 2 tablespoons olive oil
- Salt and pepper to taste

1 large prepared plank, oak or fruit wood, soaked in water (See page 13, **Plank Preparation**).

Place sliced beef in a large sealable plastic bag. Sprinkle in seasoning and massage into meat. Let sit at least 20 minutes. Place sliced vegetables in a large sealable plastic bag and coat with 2 tablespoons olive oil. Two separate bags can be used for onions and peppers if desired. Preheat a large plank on the grill or in the oven, at least 15-20 minutes. Place meat and veggies atop the plank. Grill or bake at 375° 25-30 minutes or until meat is done and vegetables are tender. Rotate food around with tongs to ensure even cooking. Serve with warm tortillas, salsa, sour cream and guacamole if desired.

RECIPE VARIATION

Chicken or pork can be substituted for beef.

Vegetable-Topped Steaks

INGREDIENTS

- 4-6 sirloin steaks or cube steaks, 1"
- Basic Beef Rub (page 50)
- 1/2 cup red pepper, chopped
- 1/2 cup green pepper, chopped
- 1/2 cup onion, chopped
- 1 tomato, chopped
- 1-2 jalapeño peppers, chopped
- Olive oil

1 prepared plank, cedar, hickory or alder, soaked in red wine or water (See page 13, **Plank Preparation**).

Sprinkle Basic Beef Rub over steaks and lightly pound with a meat mallet or tenderizing tool. Brush both sides of steaks with olive oil. In a bowl, mix peppers, onion and tomato. On a hot grill or skillet, sear steaks 30 seconds on each side. Place half of pepper mixture on a prepared plank. Place steaks atop pepper mixture and top with remaining pepper mixture. Grill or bake at 350° 20-25 minutes or until steaks reach desired doneness.

Three-Layered Pork Fillet |

INGREDIENTS

- 2-pound pork tenderloin
- 1/3 cup golden raisins
- 1/3 cup dried apricots, chopped
- 1/3 cup dates, chopped
- 2 tablespoons rum
- 2 tablespoons hot water
- 3 tablespoons butter
- 1/2 cup onion, thinly sliced
- 3 cloves garlic, minced
- 1 cup bread crumbs, plain or panko
- 1/4 teaspoon salt
- 1/4 teaspoon black pepper
- 1/8 teaspoon nutmeg
- 1 egg, beaten
- Salt and pepper to taste

1 prepared plank, alder or fruit wood, soaked in white wine or water (See page 13, **Plank Preparation**).

Prepare pork by dividing the roast into 3 equal sections, lengthwise. Lightly season with salt and pepper. Soak raisins, dates and apricots in rum and hot water. Soak until mixture cools. In a small skillet, sauté onions and garlic in butter until tender. Cool completely. In a medium mixing bowl, combine remaining ingredients. Evenly spread stuffing between two layers of pork, topping with final pork layer. Tie pork loaf together with string. Place on a prepared plank, cover with foil, tucking ends of foil 1/2" under plank to seal. Grill or bake at 375° 50-70 minutes or until internal temperature reaches 160°. Remove foil last 10 minutes of cooking time, baste with olive oil if needed. Let sit 10 minutes before slicing.

Lemon Pepper Chicken Breasts |

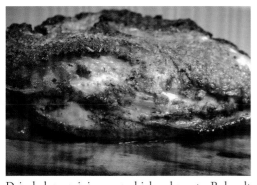

INGREDIENTS

- 4-6 chicken breasts, bone-in
- Juice of 1 lemon
- 1-2 lemons, thinly sliced
- Salt and lemon pepper to taste

1 prepared plank, alder or fruit wood, soaked in water (See page 13, **Plank Preparation**)

RECIPE VARIATION

Substitute Chicken Spice Rub (page 50) for lemon pepper or marinate in Southwestern Marinade (page 50), 2 hours prior to cooking.

Drizzle lemon juice over chicken breasts. Rub salt into chicken, lifting up skin and massaging underneath. Rub a generous amount of lemon pepper into breast meat. If desired, place a slice of lemon under skin. Place lemon slices on prepared plank. Lay seasoned chicken atop lemons. Grill or bake at 375° 45-60 minutes or until internal temperature reaches 170°. Serve chicken hot or chill and serve on chicken salad.

Twice-Cooked Ribs |

Clean any loose fat and membrane off pork ribs. Roll up and place in a crock pot on high heat. Cook 2 hours or until ribs are tender. Carefully remove ribs and place on a large prepared plank. Cover with a thin layer of rib sauce and grill or bake at 375° an additional 30 minutes or until tender. Continue to baste with rib sauce every 10 minutes. Serve with additional sauce and Mango Salsa (page 51) if desired.

RIB SAUCE PREPARATION
In a medium saucepan, sauté pepper, onion and garlic in olive oil until tender. Add remaining ingredients. Bring to a light boil and reduce heat. Simmer 10-20 minutes on low heat.

INGREDIENTS
I 1 rack pork spareribs

1 large prepared plank, hickory or pecan, soaked in vinegar or whiskey (See page 13, **Plank Preparation**).

RIB SAUCE
I 1 tablespoon olive oil
I 1 cup green pepper, diced
I 1 cup onion, diced
I 3 cloves garlic, minced
I 1 cup orange or pineapple juice
I 1/3 cup ketchup
I 1/4 cup Worcestershire sauce
I 1/4 cup cider vinegar
I 1 tablespoon brown sugar
I 1/2 teaspoon salt
I 1/4 teaspoon ground black pepper
I Dash of hot pepper sauce, if desired

Sundried Tomato Pork Loin |

In a food processor or chopper, thoroughly blend pesto ingredients. Cover pork loin with pesto and seal in a plastic zip-lock bag. Marinate 6 hours or overnight. Place seasoned pork loin on a prepared plank. Grill or bake at 375° 1 hour or until pork reaches an internal temperature of 160°. Let sit 10 minutes before slicing.

INGREDIENTS
I 1 pork loin

SUNDRIED TOMATO PESTO
I 1 8.5-ounce jar sundried tomatoes in oil
I 5 cloves garlic
I 1/3 cup parmesan cheese
I 1/2 teaspoon ground black pepper

1 prepared plank, cedar or fruit wood, soaked in water or vinegar (See page 13, **Plank Preparation**).

RECIPE VARIATION
Substitute Basil Pesto (page 51) for Sundried Tomato Pesto or marinate pork loin in Southwestern Marinade (page 50).

Herb Roasted Chicken |

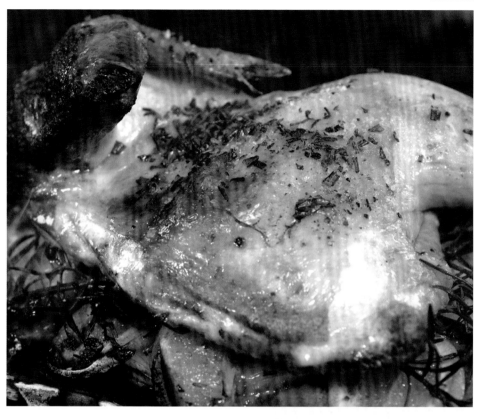

Place chicken in a medium bowl. Add olive oil, herbs, lemon juice, salt and pepper. Marinate chicken, turning occasionally, 1-6 hours. Place sliced oranges or lemons on a prepared plank. Place rosemary branches on top of oranges or lemons. Place chicken, skin side up, on top of rosemary. Grill or bake at 350° 50-60 minutes or until juices run clear and internal temperature reaches 170°. Serve with Fresh Salsa (page 51) if desired.

INGREDIENTS
- 1/2 whole chicken
- 3 tablespoons olive oil
- 1/2 tablespoon fresh rosemary, chopped
- 1/2 teaspoon fresh thyme, chopped
- Juice of 1/2 lemon
- 1 orange or lemon, sliced
- Salt and pepper to taste
- 4 rosemary branches

RECIPE VARIATION

Any combination of fresh or dried herbs can be used in this recipe. For a quick meal simply marinate chicken in prepared oil-based salad dressing of choice. Chicken pieces can be prepared using this technique.

1 prepared plank, maple or alder, soaked in white wine or water (See page 13, **Plank Preparation**).

Crunchy Chicken Strips |

Cut chicken breasts lengthwise into long strips. In a shallow dish, mix corn flakes, parmesan cheese and butter. In another shallow dish, beat eggs until frothy. In a third dish mix flour with salt and pepper. Dip chicken pieces in seasoned flour mixture, then egg, and finally into corn flake mixture. Place on a prepared plank. Grill or bake at 375° 20-25 minutes or until chicken is thoroughly cooked. Serve with Spicy Sauce (page 51) or favorite dressing.

INGREDIENTS

- 4 chicken breasts, boneless and skinless
- 1 cup finely crushed corn flakes or croutons
- 1/2 cup parmesan cheese, grated
- 2 tablespoons butter, melted
- 1/3 cup flour
- 1/2 teaspoon salt
- 1/4 teaspoon white pepper
- 1 egg, well beaten

1 prepared plank, alder or fruit wood, soaked in water (See page 13, **Plank Preparation**).

RECIPE VARIATION

Any white meat fish can be substituted for the chicken. Decrease cooking time by 5 minutes.

Greek Chicken Bake |

Cube chicken or fish into bite-sized chunks. In a large bowl mix remaining ingredients. Toss meat into vegetable mixture. Salt and pepper to taste and drizzle with olive oil. Place mixture on prepared plank. Grill or bake at 375°. Bake 20-25 minutes for fish and 30-35 minutes for chicken or until juices run clear.

INGREDIENTS

- 1-1 1/2 pounds chicken breast or fish, cubed
- 1 tomato, chopped and drained
- 1 cup green pepper, chopped
- 1 cup red onion, chopped
- 1 cup cucumber, chopped
- 10-15 kalamata olives
- 3 cloves garlic, pureed
- 1 teaspoon fresh oregano, chopped or 1/2 teaspoon dried
- 1 cup feta cheese, crumbled
- Juice and zest of 1/2 lemon
- Olive oil for drizzling
- Salt and pepper to taste

1 prepared plank, alder or fruit wood, soaked in water (See page 13, **Plank Preparation**).

Plank-Pressed Sandwiches |

INGREDIENTS

I Artisan bread
I Pesto
I Mayonnaise
I Mustard
I Horseradish
I Deli meat
I Deli cheese
I Sautéed Vegetables

1 dry plank, any wood type.

Prepare sandwiches according to taste. Brush bread with olive oil and place on a hot grill over indirect heat. Place dry plank atop sandwich and weigh down with a rock, brick or cast-iron skillet. Cook until cheese begins to melt and grill marks appear on sandwiches. Flip over and repeat on the other side.

Cajun Stuffed Pork Chops |

INGREDIENTS

I 6-8 pork chops, 1"
I 1/4 cup flour
I 2 tablespoons Cajun seasoning
I 2 tablespoons canola oil
I 1 cup onion, sliced
I 1/2 green bell pepper, sliced
I 1/2 red bell pepper, sliced
I 1-2 jalapeño peppers, seeded and sliced
I Salt and pepper to taste

1 prepared plank, hickory or cedar, soaked in water (See page 13, **Plank Preparation**).

Butterfly pork chops and open. Lightly season pork chops with salt and pepper. In a shallow dish mix flour and Cajun seasoning. Dredge all sides of chops in seasoned flour mixture. In a heavy skillet, heat canola oil on medium-high heat. Add chops and brown lightly on each side. Remove from skillet and place on prepared plank. In the same pan, add more oil and sauté onions and peppers 2-3 minutes. Sprinkle remaining seasoned flour over onion and pepper mixture. Place sautéed vegetables inside and on top of the chops. Cover with foil, tucking ends of foil 1/2" under plank to seal. Grill or bake at 375° 30-40 minutes or until internal temperature reaches 160°. Remove foil last 10 minutes of cooking time.

Fish & Seafood

Original Cedar-Planked Salmon |

INGREDIENTS

I 1 fillet of salmon or steelhead
(3-6 servings)
I 1 teaspoon Herb Medley Rub
or fish rub of choice
I Juice of 1/2 lemon
I 1 lemon, sliced
I Olive oil for brushing

1 prepared cedar plank, soaked
in water (See page 13, **Plank
Preparation**)

HERB MEDLEY RUB

I 1/2 teaspoon salt
I 1/2 teaspoon sugar
I 1/2 teaspoon dried thyme
I 1/2 teaspoon dried oregano
I 1/2 teaspoon onion powder
I 1/2 teaspoon lemon pepper
I 1/4 teaspoon dried rosemary

Place sliced lemons on prepared plank. Place fish, skin-side down on lemon layer. Squeeze 1/2 lemon over fish. Brush with olive oil and sprinkle with seasonings. Grill or bake at 375° 20-25 minutes or until fish is opaque and flakes in large chunks or reaches an internal temperature of 135°.

HERB MEDLEY RUB PREPARATION

In a small bowl, mix all rub ingredients until crushed and combined. Or using a mortar and pestle, grind until combined.

RECIPE VARIATION

There are hundreds of variations to the original cedar-planked salmon recipes. Salmon planks well with any wood flavor. Toppings can vary from Italian type seasonings to Asian flavors. Fish can be marinated prior to planking or basted during cooking time. Keeping simple ingredients to a minimum ensures the flavors of the wood smoke will come through in the final product. Don't forget that simply placing a cedar plank in the oven alongside a fillet of fish will minimize any unwanted lingering fish odors in your home.

Sour Cream & Chive Steelhead |

INGREDIENTS

- 1 fillet of steelhead or salmon (3-6 servings)
- 1 lemon
- 1/2 cup sour cream
- 2 tablespoons chives, chopped
- 1 lemon, thinly sliced
- Salt and pepper to taste

1 prepared plank, alder or fruit wood, soaked in lemon juice or water (See page 13, **Plank Preparation**).

Place fish, skin-side down, on prepared plank. Salt and pepper to taste. Spread sour cream in a thin layer over fish. Sprinkle with chives and lemon slices. Grill or bake at 375° 20-25 minutes or until fish is opaque and flakes in large chunks or reaches an internal temperature of 135°.

Artichoke-Stuffed Halibut |

INGREDIENTS

- 1 2-3-pound halibut fillet
- Salt and pepper to taste

1 prepared plank, alder or fruit wood, soaked in white wine or water (See page 13, **Plank Preparation**).

ARTICHOKE STUFFING

- 1/3 cup mayonnaise
- 1/3 cup parmesan cheese
- 1/3 cup black olives, sliced
- 2 tablespoons diced green chilies
- 1/2 cup Monterey Jack cheese
- 1 6.5-ounce jar marinated artichokes, drained and chopped

Prepare fish fillet by cutting lengthwise through the center of the fillet leaving equal thickness on top and bottom. Salt and pepper fish to taste. Fill fillet with stuffing mixture, reserving 3 tablespoons for the top. Place stuffed fillet on prepared plank. Top with additional stuffing mixture. Grill or bake at 350° 25 to 40 minutes or until fish flakes in large chunks and is no longer opaque or internal temperature reaches 140°.

ARTICHOKE STUFFING PREPARATION

In a medium bowl, gently mix all stuffing ingredients until thoroughly combined. Keep refrigerated until ready to use. This stuffing also makes a great dip on its own. Place in an ovenproof pan and baked at 350° 10 minutes. Serve with tortilla chips.

RECIPE VARIATION

A thick salmon fillet can be substituted for halibut. For a hotter filling, substitute sautéed or canned jalapeños for green chilies. Other cheeses can also be substituted.

Sesame Tuna |

Add tuna steaks to marinade and let sit 20 minutes. In a large, dry skillet, toast sesame seeds at high heat, stirring constantly for 1-2 minutes. Remove sesame seeds from hot pan immediately. Remove fish from marinade and liberally coat both sides with toasted sesame seeds. Place on a prepared plank. Grill or bake at 3750° 15-25 minutes or until fish reaches desired doneness.

INGREDIENTS
▮ 1-2 pounds tuna steaks, 3/4"
▮ 1 cup sesame seeds, toasted

1 prepared plank, alder or fruit wood, soaked in sake or water (See page 13, **Plank Preparation**).

SESAME GINGER MARINADE
▮ 1/4 cup olive oil
▮ 3 tablespoons soy sauce
▮ 2 tablespoons toasted sesame oil
▮ 2 cloves garlic, minced
▮ 1 tablespoon ginger, minced
▮ 2 teaspoons honey
▮ 1 teaspoon chili powder

SESAME GINGER MARINADE PREPARATION
In a medium bowl or sealable plastic bag, mix all marinade ingredients thoroughly.

Smokey Halibut with Salsa |

Gently massage Smokey Rub in to all sides of the halibut. Let sit 10 minutes. Place fish on prepared plank. Grill or bake at 350° 20-25 minutes or until fish flakes in large chunks and is no longer opaque or internal temperature reaches 135°. Serve with Tomatillo Salsa.

SMOKEY RUB PREPARATION
In a small bowl, mix all ingredients until thoroughly combined.

TOMATILLO SALSA PREPARATION
In a medium bowl, mix all ingredients until thoroughly combined.

INGREDIENTS
▮ 4 8-ounce halibut fillets

1 prepared plank, cedar or hickory, soaked in apple juice or water (See page 13, **Plank Preparation**).

SMOKEY RUB
▮ 1 tablespoon brown sugar
▮ 1 teaspoon fresh ground black pepper
▮ 1/2 teaspoon granulated onion
▮ 1/2 teaspoon garlic powder
▮ 1/2 teaspoon salt
▮ 1/4 teaspoon cayenne pepper
▮ 1/4 teaspoon cumin
▮ 1/4 teaspoon liquid smoke, optional

TOMATILLO SALSA
▮ 2 cups tomatillos, diced
▮ 1/2 cup onion, diced
▮ 1-2 jalapeños, seeded and diced
▮ Juice and zest of 1 lime
▮ 1/2 cup cilantro, chopped
▮ 1 tablespoon sugar
▮ Salt and pepper to taste

Curried Snapper with Peach Chutney |

In a small bowl, mix yogurt and seasonings. Coat fish and place on prepared plank. Grill or bake at 375° 20-25 minutes or until fish flakes in large chunks and is no longer opaque. Serve with warm Peach Chutney.

PEACH CHUTNEY PREPARATION

Heat olive oil in medium skillet on medium high heat. Sauté onions and peppers 10-15 minutes. Add garlic, peaches, juice and sugar. Sauté an additional 10 minutes. Remove from heat and add mint.

RECIPE VARIATION

Mango can be substituted for peaches in chutney and cilantro can be used in place of mint. Pollack, rockfish, or cod can be substituted for snapper.

INGREDIENTS
- 4 8-ounce snapper fillets
- 2/3 cup plain yogurt
- 1 teaspoon curry powder
- 1/4 teaspoon turmeric
- 1/4 teaspoon salt

1 prepared plank, alder or fruit wood, soaked in water (See page 13, **Plank Preparation**).

PEACH CHUTNEY
- 1 tablespoon olive oil
- 1/2 cup onion, finely chopped
- 1 jalapeño pepper, seeded and finely chopped
- 2 cloves garlic, crushed
- 2 large peaches, peeled and chopped
- 1/4 cup orange juice
- 1 tablespoon brown sugar
- 1/4 cup fresh mint, finely chopped

Nut-Crusted Cod |

In a shallow dish, mix flour, salt and cayenne pepper. In another shallow dish, beat egg until frothy. In a food processor or mini-chopper, finely grind nuts, coconut and bread crumbs. Coat fish with seasoned flour, dip in egg and then coat with nut mixture, pressing into fish. Place on a prepared plank. Grill or bake at 375° 20-25 minutes or until fish reaches an internal temperature of 135°. Serve with Tropical Salsa or Green Sauce (page 51), if desired.

INGREDIENTS
- 4-6 8-ounce cod fillets
- 1/2 cup macadamia and/or pistachio nuts, chopped
- 1/4 cup flaked coconut
- 1/4 cup bread crumbs
- 1 egg, beaten
- 1/4 cup flour
- 1 teaspoon salt
- 1/4 teaspoon cayenne pepper

1 prepared plank, cedar or oak, soaked water (See page 13, **Plank Preparation**).

Garlic Shrimp |

INGREDIENTS
- 1 pound shrimp, cleaned and deveined
- 1/2 cup white wine
- 1/4 cup olive oil
- 1 teaspoon Herb Medley (page 35) or seasoning of choice
- 2-4 cloves garlic, minced

Metal or wooden skewers (soak wooden skewers at least 1 hour in water)

1 prepared plank, alder or fruit wood, soaked in white wine or water, add 1 cup lemon or lime juice to water if desired (See page 13, **Plank Preparation**).

In a medium bowl, mix all seasoning ingredients. Gently toss in shrimp, coating completely. Marinate 15-20 minutes. Thread 4-6 shrimp onto each skewer. Place on prepared plank. Grill or bake at 400° 5-7 minutes or until shrimp turn pink.

RECIPE VARIATION
Prawns or scallops can be substituted for shrimp, place directly on prepared plank; skewers are not needed.

Chili-Citrus Oysters |

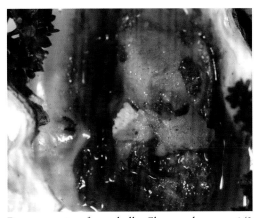

INGREDIENTS
- 20-25 oysters

2 prepared planks, oak or fruit wood, soaked in water, add 1 cup orange juice to water if desired (See page 13, **Plank Preparation**).

CHILI-CITRUS MARINADE
- 1/4 cup orange juice
- 3 tablespoons olive oil
- 1 tablespoon parsley, minced
- 1/2 teaspoon chili powder
- 1/2 teaspoon salt
- Parsley and lemon for garnish, optional

Remove oysters from shells. Clean and reserve 1/2 shell for each oyster. In a medium bowl, mix all marinade ingredients. Add shelled oysters to marinade and let sit 20 minutes, stirring occasionally. Place oysters into half-shells, spooning on 1 teaspoon of marinade. Place on prepared plank. Grill or bake at 400° 10-15 minutes or until heated through. Serve with fresh parsley and lemon slices.

Desserts

Triple Berry Tart |

INGREDIENTS

- 1 prepared pie crust
- 1 cup blueberries
- 1 cup raspberries
- 1 cup strawberries, stemmed and quartered
- 1/2 cup sugar
- 1/4 cup flour
- 1/2 teaspoon cinnamon
- 3 tablespoons butter

1 prepared plank, maple or fruit wood, soaked in water (See page 13, **Plank Preparation**).

In a medium bowl, mix flour and sugar. Add berries, gently tossing to coat. Preheat prepared plank at 400° for 15-20 minutes. Place crust on hot plank and quickly place berries in the middle of the crust. Shape crust up over berries, leaving an opening on top. Divide butter into 3-4 pats and place atop berries. Due to possible dripping, place plank on a cookie sheet or foil base to catch any sugary drips. Grill or bake at 400° 35-40 minutes or until crust is golden brown. If a crispy crust is desired, finish tart on a hot pizza stone for the final 10 minutes of cooking time.

RECIPE VARIATION

Any seasonal berries can be used for this dessert. If only using blueberries or blackberries, add 1 tablespoon lemon juice to fruit mixture. For Strawberry Rhubarb Tart, increase sugar to 3/4 cup.

Apple Crumble |

Place sliced apples in a large mixing bowl. Add sugar, flour and cinnamon, stirring just to evenly coat slices. Arrange apples in an even layer over prepared plank. Leave at least a 1/2 inch of plank space around the edges. Sprinkle crumble topping evenly over apples. Due to possible dripping, place plank on a cookie sheet or foil base to catch any sugary drips. Grill or bake at 375° 25-30 minutes or until apples are tender and crust is golden brown. Serve with ice cream.

CRUMBLE TOPPING PREPARATION
In a medium bowl, mix dry ingredients. Cut butter into mixture and crumble with a fork.

INGREDIENTS
- 3 tart apples, thinly sliced
- 1/4 cup sugar
- 2 tablespoons flour
- 1 teaspoon cinnamon

1 prepared plank, maple or fruit wood, soaked in apple juice or water (See page 13, **Plank Preparation**).

CRUMBLE TOPPING
- 1/3 cup oatmeal
- 1/3 cup brown sugar
- 2 tablespoons flour
- 1/3 cup butter, softened

RECIPE VARIATION
Walnuts, pecans and/or raisins make a nice addition to this dessert. Rhubarb can be used in place of apples, increase sugar to 3/4 cup.

Toffee-Topped Pound Cake |

INGREDIENTS
- 1 pound cake, sliced 1/2"
- 1/2 cup chocolate toffee bar pieces
- 4 ounces cream cheese, softened
- 2 tablespoons butter, softened

1 prepared plank, alder or fruit wood, soaked in water (See page 13, **Plank Preparation**).

In a medium bowl, combine toffee pieces, cream cheese and butter. Spread toffee mixture evenly onto pound cake slices. Place on prepared plank. Grill or bake at 400° 8-12 minutes, until toffee mixture is lightly browned.

Wrap It!

Cedar-Wrapped Teriyaki Salmon |

INGREDIENTS
- 4 6-8 ounce skinless salmon fillets
- Teriyaki Marinade (page 50)

4 prepared cedar grilling papers,
(See page 12, **Wrap Preparation**).

Marinate fish in marinade at least 20 minutes. Place papers on a flat surface and put fish in the middle. Fold papers with the grain and close, securing with a metal paper clip or heat-resistant band. Place filled papers on a baking sheet and bake in a preheated, 375° oven, or on a hot grill using indirect heat. Cook 15 minutes or until fish flakes in large chunks and is no longer opaque.

Cherry-Wrapped Scallops |

INGREDIENTS
- 9-12 scallops
- 2 tablespoons fresh parsley, finely chopped
- 2 tablespoons fresh chives, finely chopped
- 2 tablespoons fresh basil, finely chopped
- Juice of 1 lime
- 1/4 teaspoon salt

4 prepared cherry grilling papers,
(See page 12, **Wrap Preparation**).

In a medium bowl, gently mix all ingredients. Marinate 10-15 minutes. Place papers on a flat surface, put scallops down the middle. Fold papers with the grain and close, securing with a metal paper clip or heat-resistant band. Place filled papers on a baking sheet and bake in a preheated, 375° oven, or on a hot grill using indirect heat. Cook 8-10 minutes or until scallops are slightly firm.

Alder-Wrapped Cilantro Lime Shrimp |

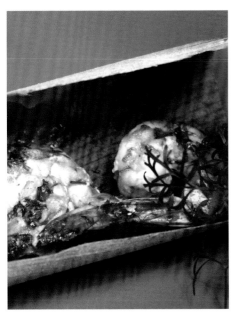

INGREDIENTS
I 1 pound raw shrimp
I Juice and zest from 1-2 limes
I 1 tablespoon soy sauce
I 1 tablespoon peanut oil
I 1/4 cup fresh cilantro, chopped

4-6 prepared grilling papers, (See page 12, **Wrap Preparation**).

Shell and devein shrimp. In a medium bowl, mix remaining ingredients, add shrimp and marinate 15 minutes, tossing occasionally. Place papers on a flat surface and evenly distribute shrimp down the middle. Fold papers with the grain and close, securing with a metal paper clip or heat-resistant band. Place filled papers on a baking sheet and bake in a preheated, 375° oven, or on a hot grill using indirect heat. Cook 6-10 minutes or until shrimp turns pink. Fish chunks can be substituted for the shrimp. Add at least 5 minutes to cooking time for fish.

Cedar-Wrapped Fish & Vegetables |

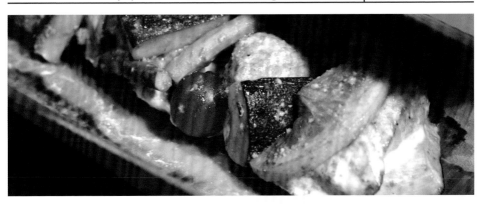

Place paper on a flat surface and evenly distribute all ingredients down the middle. Fold paper, with the grain, and close, securing with a metal paper clip or heat-resistant band. Place filled paper on a baking sheet and bake in a preheated, 350° oven, or on a hot grill using indirect heat. Cook 12-15 minutes or until fish reaches desired doneness.

INGREDIENTS
I 6 ounces skinless fish, cubed
I 2-4 cubes zucchini
I 1 stalk asparagus, chopped
I 1/2 tomato, chopped
I 1 clove garlic, minced
I 1 slice lemon
I 1 tablespoon melted butter
I Salt and pepper to taste

1 prepared cedar grilling paper, (See page 12, **Wrap Preparation**).

Alder-Wrapped Chicken Breast |

INGREDIENTS
- 1 pound boneless, skinless chicken breasts
- 2 tablespoons olive oil
- 4 cloves garlic, minced
- Juice and zest from 1 lemon
- 1/4 cup fresh parsley leaves
- 1 tablespoon fresh rosemary and/or thyme
- Salt and pepper to taste

4-6 prepared alder grilling papers, (See page 12, **Wrap Preparation**).

Cut chicken into long strips. In a medium bowl, mix remaining ingredients, add chicken and marinate up to 30 minutes, tossing occasionally. Place papers on a flat surface and evenly distribute chicken down the middle. Fold papers with the grain and close, securing with a metal paper clip or heat-resistant band. Place filled papers on a baking sheet and bake in a preheated, 375° oven, or on a hot grill using indirect heat. Cook 15-20 minutes or until chicken has reached an internal temperature of 165°.

Flat-Wrap Halibut |

INGREDIENTS
- 1 12-ounce halibut fillet
- 2 tablespoons butter, melted
- 2 tablespoons parsley, chopped
- 2 cloves garlic, pureed
- 9 slices zucchini
- Salt and pepper to taste

1 prepared cedar grilling paper, (See page 12, **Wrap Preparation**).

In a small bowl combine butter, parsley and garlic. Place zucchini slices on prepared wrap. Salt and pepper to taste. Place fish atop zucchini layer and cover with parsley mixture. Place wrap, flat, on a preheated hot grill over indirect heat. Cook 25-35 minutes or until fish flakes in large chunks and is no longer opaque or reaches an internal temperature of 140°.

Maple Chili Pork with Black Bean Salad |

INGREDIENTS

- 1 pound pork loin or chicken breast, cubed
- 1 15-ounce can black beans, drained
- 1 4-ounce can diced green chilies
- 1 cup bell pepper, chopped
- 1/2 cup corn
- 1/2 cup red onion, chopped
- 1 large tomato, chopped
- 2 cloves garlic, minced
- 1 tablespoon olive oil
- 2 teaspoons white wine vinegar
- 2 tablespoons Chili Rub (page 50) or prepared taco seasoning

4-6 prepared maple grilling papers, (See page 12, **Wrap Preparation**).

Place Chili Rub or taco seasoning in a sealable plastic bag. Drop meat into bag and massage, let sit 10 minutes. In a medium bowl gently combine all salad ingredients, vinegar and olive oil. Place papers on a flat surface and evenly distribute black bean mixture down the middle. Place marinated meat atop the black bean mixture. Fold papers with the grain and close, securing with a metal paper clip or heat-resistant band. Place filled papers on a baking sheet and bake in a preheated, 375° oven, or on a hot grill using indirect heat. Cook 20-25 minutes or until pork has reached desired doneness.

Cherry-Wrapped Trout with Herbs |

INGREDIENTS

- 4-8 small trout
- 1 pint cherry tomatoes, chopped
- 1 bunch fresh parsley
- 1 bunch fresh cilantro
- 1 bunch fresh mint
- 4 rosemary branches
- Salt and pepper to taste

4 prepared cherry grilling papers, (See page 12, **Wrap Preparation**).

Place papers on a flat surface and put fish in the middle, going with the grain. Salt and pepper fish both inside and out. Evenly distribute herbs and tomatoes among each wrap. Tuck herbs under and into fish. Fold papers with the grain and close, securing with a metal paper clip or heat-resistant band. Place filled papers on a baking sheet and bake in a preheated, 375° oven, or on a hot grill using indirect heat. Cook 15-25 minutes or until fish flakes in large chunks and is no longer opaque.

Coconut-Coated Stone-Fruit Wraps |

INGREDIENTS
- 2-3 cups stone fruit, any combination of the following:
  peaches, peeled and chopped
  apricots, peeled and chopped
  plums, chopped cherries, pitted
- 1/4 cup Grand Marnier
- 1/4 teaspoon cinnamon
- 1/8 teaspoon salt
- 1 cup sweetened flaked coconut

In a large bowl, combine Grand Marnier, cinnamon and salt. Add stone fruit combination of choice and gently toss, coating all fruit. Let sit at least 20 minutes. Gently roll each piece of fruit in coconut. Place papers on a flat surface and evenly distribute fruit down the middle. Fold papers with the grain and close, securing with a metal paper clip or heat-resistant band. Place filled papers on a baking sheet and bake in a preheated, 375° oven, or on a hot grill using indirect heat. Bake 10-15 minutes or until fruit is heated through. Serve with Cheesecake Cream or ice cream.

4-6 prepared alder, maple or cherry grilling papers, (See page 12, **Wrap Preparation**).

CHEESECAKE CREAM
- 4 ounces cream cheese, softened
- 1/3 cup sour cream
- 1 cup powdered sugar
- 1 tablespoon fresh lemon juice
- 1 teaspoon real vanilla

CHEESECAKE CREAM PREPARATION
In a medium bowl, blend all ingredients until smooth.

Maple-Wrapped S'mores |

INGREDIENTS
- 4 2"x2" brownies, quartered
- 40 mini-marshmallows
- 2/3 cup graham cracker crumbs
- 1/2 toasted almonds, finely chopped

4 prepared maple grilling papers, (See page 12, **Wrap Preparation**).

Place papers on a flat surface. Sprinkle graham cracker crumbs down the middle of the wrap, going with the grain. Evenly top with brownies, marshmallows and almonds. Fold papers with the grain and close, securing with a metal paper clip or heat-resistant band. Place filled papers on a baking sheet and bake in a preheated, 375° oven, or on a hot grill using indirect heat. Cook 5-10 minutes or until brownies are warm and marshmallows begin to melt.

Marinades, Rubs & More

Chicken Spice Rub

- 1 tablespoon chili powder
- 2 teaspoons dried cumin
- 2 teaspoons dried coriander
- 1 teaspoon salt
- 1/2 teaspoon dry mustard
- 1/2 teaspoon dried oregano
- 1/2 teaspoon ground black pepper
- 1/4 teaspoon cayenne pepper

In a small bowl, mix all rub ingredients until thoroughly combined.

Southwestern Marinade

INGREDIENTS

- 1 can beer
- 1 red onion, thinly sliced
- 1 jalapeño pepper, thinly sliced
- 1/2 cup lime juice
- 1/2 cup fresh cilantro, chopped
- 2 tablespoons olive oil
- 1 tablespoon lime zest, optional
- 1/2 teaspoon salt
- 1/2 teaspoon black pepper
- 1/2 teaspoon red pepper flakes
- 1/2 teaspoon ground cumin

In a medium bowl, mix all sauce ingredients until thoroughly combined.

Chili Rub

INGREDIENTS

- 1 teaspoon salt
- 1 teaspoon ground coriander
- 1 teaspoon garlic powder
- 1 teaspoon chili powder
- 1/2 teaspoon white pepper
- 1/2 teaspoon ground cumin
- 1/2 teaspoon granulated garlic

In a small bowl, mix all rub ingredients until thoroughly combined.

Teriyaki Marinade

INGREDIENTS

- 1/4 cup soy sauce
- 1/4 cup cream sherry
- 1/4 cup olive oil
- 3 tablespoons shallot or green onion, finely chopped
- 1 tablespoon brown sugar
- 1 inch ginger root, peeled and grated

In a small bowl, mix all sauce ingredients until thoroughly combined.

Basic Beef Rub

INGREDIENTS

- 2 teaspoons granulated garlic
- 1 teaspoon granulated onion
- 1 teaspoon brown sugar
- 1 teaspoon ground black pepper

In a small bowl, mix all rub ingredients until thoroughly combined.

Rosemary Balsamic Marinade

INGREDIENTS

- 1/2 cup olive oil
- 1/4 cup balsamic vinegar
- 2 teaspoons brown sugar
- 1 tablespoon garlic, pureed
- 1/2 teaspoon fresh or dried rosemary, chopped
- 1/2 teaspoon salt
- 1/2 teaspoon black pepper

In a small bowl, mix all sauce ingredients until thoroughly combined.

Tropical Salsa |

INGREDIENTS

- 1 green banana, peeled and chopped
- 1 cup pineapple, finely chopped
- 1 mango, chopped
- 2 tablespoons fresh cilantro, chopped
- 2 tablespoons fresh mint, chopped, optional
- 2 teaspoons fresh ginger, minced
- 2 teaspoons Asian chili sauce, optional
- 1/2 teaspoon salt

In a medium bowl, gently mix all ingredients. Refrigerate at least 30 minutes before serving.

Mango Salsa |

INGREDIENTS

- 2 cups mango, cubed
- 1 red bell pepper, finely chopped
- 2 green onions, chopped
- 1/4 cup cilantro leaves, chopped
- Juice of 1 lime
- 1 tablespoon ginger, minced
- 1 tablespoon brown sugar
- 1 tablespoon fish sauce, optional
- 2-3 teaspoons chili sauce

In a medium bowl, gently toss all ingredients until combined. Refrigerate, at least 30 minutes before serving.

Fresh Salsa |

INGREDIENTS

- 6 roma-style tomatoes, chopped
- 1/2 cup bell pepper, chopped
- 1/2 cup onion, diced
- 2 jalapeño peppers, diced
- 2 tablespoons lemon or lime juice
- 1 teaspoon sugar
- 1/2 teaspoon salt
- 1/2 teaspoon cumin
- 1/2 teaspoon chili powder
- Black pepper to taste
- Hot pepper sauce to taste, optional

In a medium bowl, gently toss all ingredients until combined.

Basil Pesto |

INGREDIENTS

- 1 1/2 cups basil leaves
- 2 cloves garlic
- 1/4 cup toasted pine nuts
- 1/2 cup parmesan cheese, grated
- 2 tablespoons extra virgin olive oil
- Salt and pepper to taste

In a food processor or mini-chopper, blend all ingredients until thoroughly combined.

Spicy Sauce |

INGREDIENTS

- 3 tablespoons ketchup
- 1 tablespoon hot sauce or sambal
- 1 teaspoon granulated garlic
- 1 teaspoon granulated onion
- 1 teaspoon white sugar
- 1 teaspoon cider vinegar
- 1/2 teaspoon red pepper flakes

In a small bowl, mix all sauce ingredients until thoroughly combined.

Green Sauce |

INGREDIENTS

- 1 cup fresh cilantro leaves
- Juice from 2 lemons
- 2 tablespoons sugar
- 2 cloves garlic
- 2 large jalapeños, seeded and chopped
- 1/4 cup walnut pieces
- 1/2 teaspoon salt

In a food processor or mini-chopper, blend all ingredients until thoroughly combined.

Index

Index

Recipe Notes

About the author

With a focus on healthy, creative meals that are easy to prepare, Tiffany Haugen is fast becoming a recognized and respected cookbook author and columnist. A major in health education, combined with a Masters Degree and several years of public school teaching, has helped shape Tiffany into the inspirational cookbook author she is today.

Her cooking skills stem from a lifetime of practical experience. Tiffany grew up with a passion for cooking. As an adult she has traveled to nearly 30 countries, and lived in such exotic places as Alaska's Arctic, Indonesia and Spain, where she cooked extensively with local foods. The background she's gained continues to stimulate her worldly approach on simple food preparation.

Having coauthored a variety of best-selling cookbooks on topics such as plank cooking, smoke-cooking, wild game, fish and more, this book echoes Tiffany's easy-to-follow style.

Tiffany Haugen lives with her husband, Scott, and two sons Braxton and Kazden, in western Oregon.

GRILL IT! Plank It! Smoke It! *by Tiffany Haugen*

With recipes taken directly from her series of books on grilling, planking and smoking, Tiffany Haugen has put everything together in one piece of work. Adding to these creations is a bonus section containing nearly 100 recipes for marinades, rubs, sauces, salsas and more. Full color; 6 x 9; 156 pages.

Spiral SB: $24.95
ISBN-13: 978-1-57188-416-9
UPC: 0-81127-00250-4

COOKING SALMON & STEELHEAD
Exotic Recipes From Around the World
by Scott & Tiffany Haugen

Globe-trotting authors, Scott and Tiffany Haugen share some of the world's most exquisite flavors in this book. Whether selecting your fish at the market or catching it yourself, *Cooking Salmon & Steelhead* teaches you what to look for, how to care for your fish and offers unique and insightful ways to prepare this healthy meat.

Spiral SB: $24.95

ISBN: 1-57188-291-X

SMOKING SALMON & STEELHEAD
by Scott & Tiffany Haugen

With over 50 wet and dry brine recipes and tips on how to handle and prepare your fish, this book is packed with valuable information. With original recipes created by the authors to secret recipes gathered from fishing guides and seasoned anglers, there's something in this book for everyone. 6 x 9 inches; 96 pages, all-color.

Spiral SB: $19.95   **ISBN: 1-57188-290-1**

COOKING BIG GAME
by Scott & Tiffany Haugen

Game meat is one of the most nutritious forms of protein, and the Haugens, having lived a subsistence lifestyle, offer innovative twists in preparing big game. From family favorites to tastes the world over, more than 100 imaginative recipes will have you clearing your freezer in no time.

Spiral SB: $19.95

ISBN: 1-57188-407-7

UPC: 0-81127-00241-2

PLANK COOKING: THE ESSENCE OF NATURAL WOOD
by Scott & Tiffany Haugen

From the oven to the grill, plank cooking has made its mark in the culinary world. This book outlines how to master the art of plank cooking, from seasoning planks, choosing woods to detailed cooking tips in over 100 easy-to-follow recipes. Full color; 6 x 9; 152 pages

Spiral SB: $19.95
ISBN: 1-57188-332-0